AF660909

the kid books

Dadu takes me to GURUDWARA

Author
Tanvi Nishchal
Illustrator
Charul Saini

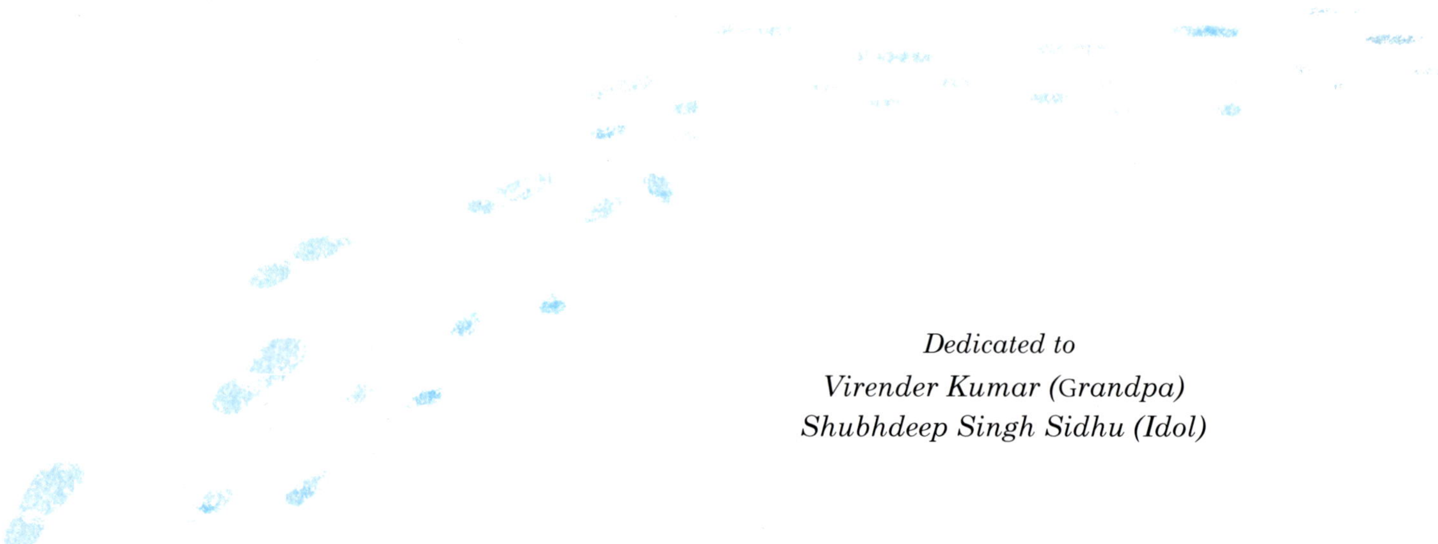

Dedicated to

Virender Kumar (Grandpa)

Shubhdeep Singh Sidhu (Idol)

Tag along with Mahi as she visits

Gurudwara for the first time

with her best buddy,

Dadu and how he answers her whats and whys

Sat Sri Akal to all!

Welcome to my channel. Hope everyone is doing well. Today I am very excited. I am taking my best friend, my lovely granddaughter, to a very special place for the first time. ....”

“Dadu hurry up, we are getting late.” Shouted Mahi.

“.. you heard her, see you all,” He paused the video and went outside.

"Dadu where are we going today?" asked Mahi.

"You will have to answer a riddle for this.

Are you ready?" said Dadu.

"Yes" she clapped excitedly.

"Saves us from rain and fire,
We make it our own,
And live with our family,
And we all call it ......?"

m m m
m m m

"Home!!"
answered Mahi

"Yes! Very good! Today we are going to God's Home.

After reaching Mahi asked,

"Dadu, why do all people cover their head?."

"Beta ji God loves us all
So we cover our heads
Because in God's home
No one is big or small."

Mahi picks a patka of her favourite colour green out of the pile. Dadu helps her to tie it around her head.

“Dadu what are they doing?”.

Asked Mahi pointing at the direction of people praying.

“What do you do when you can’t solve a sum?” asked Dadu.

“I go and ask mum.” answered Mahi.

“If mummy is not there then who will help you?” asked Dadu.

“I take Papa ji’s phone and google the sum.” answered Mahi.

"God is busy, he has to go here and there,

So, he made this book, Just like Google,

So you can find all your answers here" Explained Dadu.

"Really! It has all the solutions?" her eyes glazed with wonder.

"Yes, beta ji, God has given all the answers to all of your questions in this book."

They bowed their heads.

“Dadu what are we going to do in this big wide room?” asked Mahi as her eyes went around slowly to get a glance of the entire hall.

“Well, Mahi when someone comes to our house how do we treat them?” asked Dadu.

“We offer them samosas and chai and we greet them.” answered Mahi with glee

Yes, very good so when in God’s home

He loves to feed us all

Everyone sits in rows

At the langar hall.

Dadu what are they doing?
she pointed out to the people.

An elderly sardar ji was cooking dal

A Sardarni was making rotis

Another Sardar ji was peeling vegetables

"Good question, Mahi, remember when Dadi's head was in pain What did you do then?" asked Dadu.

"I sat on her bed rub some balm on her forehead." Mahi said, *"And then?" Dadu asked "She gave me toffies and chocolates One for me and one for my classmate."* Said Mahi.

"So, if you do anything good on your own
God becomes very happy with you
He give you lots of gift and blessings too."

Just then, Dadu stopped to talk to an old kin
Noticing Mahi was not next to him Until he
saw her handing out rotis in the kitchen
He smiled, wiping a tear then.

DID YOU KNOW?

Khanda – A double edged sword that shows belief in one God.

Gurumukhi – Means coming from Guru's mouth and was invented by second Guru Angad Dev.

Baaz – A hawk representing qualities of a true Sikh

Langar – A community kitchen started by Guru Nanak, first guru and founder of Sikhism.

Tanvi Nishchal has been writing since she was a mere teenager. She has a Master's degree in English. Writing is oxygen for her as it is only through words, she is able to express herself.

Her mantra for writing is that to write well one needs to be an avid reader. Her short stories have also been published in books such as Born too Soon and existing loudly.

@trandomryme

Charul Saini is drawing and painting ever since she could remember and believes that she will continue to do so till her last breath. She believes being creative comes naturally to everyone, it is staying creative that requires discipline and consistency.

@charulsaini

An Imprint of Unbound Script

Dadu takes me to Gurudwara
First Edition - Nov, 2024

ISBN : 978-81-19745-23-4

© Tanvi Nishchal 2024

Publisher : **Unbound Script**
2/41, Ansari Road,
Daryaganj, Delhi - 110002
E-mail : books@unboundscript.com
Website : www.unboundscript.com
Phone : 011-35807601

DADU TAKES ME TO GURUDWARA
Written *by* Tanvi Nishchal
Illustrated *by* Charul Saini

Printed in India

Price: ₹ 149/-

All Rights reserved. No part of this book may be reproduced or used in any manner without written permission of the copyright owner except for the use of quotations in a book review.